Original title:
A Christmas Wrapped in Wonder

Copyright © 2024 Creative Arts Management OÜ
All rights reserved.

Author: Atticus Thornton
ISBN HARDBACK: 978-9916-94-072-3
ISBN PAPERBACK: 978-9916-94-073-0

A Journey of Heartfelt Wishes

In a town where snowflakes waltz and spin,
Santa's sleigh gets stuck, oh where to begin?
Elves giggle as they pull with all their might,
While Rudolph rolls his eyes, what a silly sight!

Mittens hang from rooftops, not a chimney in sight,
One cat thinks it's cozy, lays down for the night.
The cookies left out? Well, they've all disappeared,
Squirrel has run off, with a grin, oh so weird!

Tinsel tangled in a green, feathery mess,
Mom shouts with laughter, oh what a right mess!
The dog steals the wreath, thinking it's meant to chew,
While grandma shakes her head, her cookies flew too!

Lights twinkle above, a clip clop is heard,
Look out, it's the llama, wearing a festive beard!
A parade of bright wishes, a giggle, a cheer,
Celebrating the joy that's spreading far and near!

Wishes Cradled in Snow

Snowflakes dance like tiny sprites,
Hitching rides on furry heights.
The snowman wears my scarf so bright,
I think he just might take a flight!

Laughter echoes through the night,
As sledding plans take off in flight.
With hot cocoa, a frothy delight,
We'll toast to fun with pure delight.

The Joyous Chime of Bells

Jingle bells announce a race,
Runny noses, a silly face!
Every sound is out of place,
Even Grandma's awkward pace!

Chiming notes fill the chilly air,
Cats in bows, do they really care?
As carols clash, a crazy flair,
We laugh until we lose our hair!

Enchanted Moments Beneath the Tree

Presents piled with endless cheer,
Dad's snoring, can we keep it clear?
A cat's tangled 'round the deer,
Oops! I think I've lost my beer!

Twinkling lights do strange things too,
Grandpa's wig, a sparkly view.
As shadows spin, a waltz anew,
We dance in chaos—who knew?

Frost-Kissed Memories

Frosty windows bear a tale,
Of snowball fights that will prevail.
A warm-up plan? Hot soup in a pail,
But first, we'll sled like we're on a whale!

Grandma's cookies, a sugary win,
But watch the cat, not to let him in!
A battle rages for that last tin,
As laughter spills, all joys begin.

Pine Needle Perfume and Comfort

The tree smells like a grand estate,
With needles sharp enough to grate.
Presents piled up to the ceiling,
Underneath, the cat's congealing.

Eggnog spills on the floor with flair,
The dog sneaks in, without a care.
A festive dance, a clumsy spin,
Sure hope that nobody's wearing skin!

Secrets Held by the Winter Winds

The wind whispers tales of snowball fights,
Of mittens lost on frosty nights.
Children plotting tricks on their peers,
While sipping cocoa, drowning their fears.

A snowman grins, but he's held up by hope,
Wrapped tight in charms and a red wool rope.
Lost my hat in this frozen mess,
Now I'm a fashionably snowy guess!

Glowing Faces and Frosty Wishes

Faces aglow with joy and cheer,
Some with food stains, oh dear!
The cookies are shaped like jolly elves,
But mostly look like deformed shelves.

Hot cocoa rivers, milky and sweet,
Tasting like childhood with every beat.
Laughter echoes in the frosty air,
Remind me again, who brought that chair?

Whispers of Warmth Amidst the Chill

Under blankets piled like a mountain tall,
We discover holiday snacks and brawl.
Grandma's quilt is a mystery of thread,
Each patch a secret of things we dread.

Outside it snows, a winter show,
We're stuck inside with nowhere to go.
Let's hang up socks, mix fluff with cheer,
And hope Santa's sleigh doesn't shift a gear!

Frosted Trails of the Past

In the snow, we tripped and slid,
Waving at the neighborhood kid.
Frosty socks, can't feel my toes,
Laughing louder as the cold wind blows.

Sledding down the icy hill,
Who knew that we'd spill?
With every tumble, every fall,
We rang out with joy, oh what a call!

Stars Above, Joy Below

Twinkling lights on the tree,
I swear I saw a deer flee!
Great Aunt Hilda lost her hat,
Now the cat thinks she's a mat!

Up above, the stars wink bright,
While we wage our pillow fight.
Mother yells, 'Now settle down!'
As we wear her best nightgown!

A Tangle of Holiday Dreams

Ribbon and bows in a crazy mess,
I can't even find the Christmas dress!
Baking cookies? Dough is on my face,
Look out, the flour's a wild chase!

A tree that leans like it's had a drink,
Ornaments hang by the merest link.
We laugh until we nearly cry,
As the cat executes a fly-by!

The Call of the Winter Eve

Santa's list went lost, oh dear,
Had he dropped it right here?
Rudolph's nose lights up the night,
But the dog thinks it's a flashlight!

Snowmen with faces all askew,
They're rolling their eyes at me too.
What a sight, this winter eve,
Just wait 'til I try to weave!

Carols that Break the Silence

In the town square carolers find,
A choir of cats, quite unrefined.
They meow in tune, but it's quite absurd,
Their harmonies lost, no one's heard.

Snowflakes dance on a park bench seat,
While squirrels steal snacks, oh what a feat!
With jingle bells stuck on a fawn,
The laughter erupts, as chaos goes on.

Shimmering Paths of Joy and Wonder

With glitter sprinkled on gingerbread men,
They march in line, oh such good friends!
But icing melts in the winter sun,
And now they're just a gooey run.

The lights twinkle like stars on gin,
As dogs in sweaters try to get in.
They race and chase, what a funny sight,
One jumps in the snow, oh what a plight!

The Gift of Presence and Reflection

Unwrap the joy, that's the big deal,
But wait, it's just a giant pickle meal!
Laughter erupts, as we take a bite,
Who knew brine could bring so much light?

A lamp with socks all mismatched and bright,
Gives off a glow, oh what a sight!
A gift of the past, what a rich layer,
Old Uncle Bob's forgotten prayer.

Cherished Dreams in Glacial Bliss

Snowmen wobble with carrot for a nose,
But a bird steals it—oh, heaven knows!
The snowball fight heats up with flair,
Except it's just snowflakes in the air.

Ice skates twirl on a pond that's thin,
As grandpa slips, and dizzily spins.
Laughter echoes, it's all in fun,
As we chase the light of the winter sun.

A Night Beneath the Starglow

Beneath the twinkling sky so bright,
Santa's reindeer took a flight.
They flew in circles, what a sight,
While elves were singing with delight.

The snowmen danced, all out of place,
One tripped and fell; oh, what a chase!
Hot cocoa spilled, a creamy race,
Winter's joy took center space.

In pajamas, we gave a cheer,
Mom forgot the cookies, oh dear!
Dad wore antlers, looking weird,
Laughter filled the chilly sphere.

With every giggle, spirits soared,
This night of wonder we adored.
While pup tried to munch on the cord,
We fell asleep, blissfully floored.

Reflections of Holiday Cheer

Reflections in the window pane,
Show kids outside, causing pain.
They're making snowmen with a stain,
A carrot nose, oh, what a gain!

Grandpa's hat is on the tree,
What's Christmas without irony?
A squirrel stole the sparkly glee,
No gifts remain just misery!

A mistletoe hung just too low,
Someone slipped on ice — a no-go.
We laughed so hard, couldn't say no,
What memories, that's all we know.

We sang songs to the festive beat,
With Auntie dancing on her feet.
Her moves, I must admit, are sweet,
This holiday is quite the treat!

Golden Moments in the Frost

Oh look, a raccoon in a hat,
He swipes the snacks and scurries fat.
We chase him down with a loud "splatt!"
Then trip on snow, our plans go flat.

The fire crackles, hot dogs roast,
As we recall the ghostly boast.
Last year's turkey, oh, what a host,
But laughter's what we cherish most.

Dad's in charge of lights this year,
He tangled cords, what a great fear!
But when they lit, we cheered, hooray!
He winked and grinned in grand display.

With every giggle, warmth did rise,
As snowflakes danced down from the skies.
We wrapped up in our warm disguise,
With golden moments, oh, such highs!

The Enchantment in the Air

The sky is filled with jolly cheer,
A cat in boots draws every sneer.
We watched him leap, it was unclear,
Did he come down to steer the deer?

Singing carols, we made a mess,
Eggnog spilled; oh, what a stress!
The cat now thinks he's dressed to impress,
As we pulled together our best guess.

A snowball fight breaks out nearby,
One aimed too high; oh my, oh my!
The neighbor squealed and started to cry,
While laughter rang and spirits did fly.

In this season of silly delight,
We cherish moments, pure and bright.
With friends and family, hearts take flight,
The air is magic, what a sight!

Light in the Whispering Snow

Snowflakes whisper, soft and light,
They dance around, a joyous sight.
Elves are slipping, oh what a show,
Tripping over their big red bows.

Hot cocoa spills in a clumsy cheer,
Marshmallows float like little deer.
A snowman winks with a carrot nose,
And giggles when the wind just blows.

Enchanted Nights of December

Under twinkling lights we prance,
A festive dance, what a silly chance!
The cat in the tree, quite a sight to see,
Swatting at ornaments, oh let it be!

Frosty's hat flies up with a whoosh,
He shouts, "Catch me!" and starts to swoosh.
We chase him down, bundled so tight,
In a giggle-fest that lasts all night.

Tinsel and Twinkling Stars

Tinsel sparkles, a shiny mess,
Caught in hair, oh what a dress!
The dog in a scarf, it's quite the look,
He thinks he's starring in a storybook.

Cookies vanish, a mysterious crime,
We leave out treats, not a single dime.
Santa's laugh echoes, such a tease,
"Who ate them all?" he asks with ease.

A Tapestry of Joy

Lights are tangled, a garish sight,
We laugh and tug, what a silly fight!
The spirit's here, full of cheer,
As we hang the lights, shedding a tear.

Gift paper rips like a hungry beast,
Oh no! It's out of control, at least!
Socks for Aunt May and a toy for Ted,
Watch a surprise jump from the bed.

Giggles echo through the night,
Each little moment feels just right.
With laughter and joy, we carry on,
Wrapping fun 'til the break of dawn.

A Symphony of Season's Greetings

Jingle bells in the air, loud and bright,
Santa's sleigh zooms out of sight!
Reindeer prance with style and grace,
Wearing that silly, funny face.

Tables piled high with treats galore,
Grandma's cookies, who could ask for more?
Gifts wrapped tight with ribbons unspooled,
We laugh as the paper gets overruled!

Snowmen wobble with carrot noses,
Hats so big, they're hiding roses!
Neighbors carol with off-key notes,
Even the dogs join with funny quotes!

Merriment blooms from our funny quirks,
Who knew joy could come with such jerks?
Sipping cocoa as snowflakes dance,
Winter fun is our happy chance!

Journey through a Winter Wonderland

Fluffy clouds of snow drift down,
Boys and girls spin round and round.
A sled goes by, with shouts of glee,
While the snowflakes laugh, 'Come sled with me!'

Jackets pop open, with zippers unzipped,
Snowballs fly, while hot cocoa's sipped.
Frosty fingers and chilly toes,
But still, we grin, and strike funny poses!

Igloos made from packed-up white,
Snowball fights that last all night.
Everyone slips, and then they land,
In a heap, like a band of sand!

We'll write our names in the snow so bright,
Watching them melt, it's quite a sight!
From snowmen's hats to jolly cheers,
This snowy caper spans the years!

The Hush of Snowfall at Dusk

Dusk falls softly, the air is still,
Snowflakes dance with a funny thrill.
Children giggle, their cheeks aglow,
While sipping tea as the wind starts to blow.

Pajamas flair like a wild parade,
As children dream in a snowy glade.
Sleds forgotten, tucked in a pile,
We bounce on couches, all with a smile!

Whispers of mischief fill the air,
While shadows flicker like they don't care.
Scents of cookies drift through the night,
Sniffing around, we plot our delight.

Lights twinkle softly from every street,
As neighbors share goodies, oh what a treat!
The laughter builds, and the joy ignites,
In this winter hush, our fun takes flight!

Hearths alight with Holiday Spirit

By the fire, we gather near,
Telling tales while sipping beer.
Funny stories make us chuckle,
As we roast marshmallows on the hustle!

Ornaments hang, bright and bold,
One fell down, it shattered gold.
Gifts exchanged with oops and oohs,
Wrapped with laughter and funny shoes!

Cookie plates left bare and clean,
Santa's belly bulging at the seam.
Merry chaos fills the air,
With silly socks gracing each chair.

Family ruckus, the joyful noise,
We cheer together, with all our toys.
As laughter echoes into the night,
Our hearts alight with pure delight!

The Heart of Winter's Glow

In the heart of winter's glow,
Snowmen dance, put on a show.
With carrot noses, funny hats,
Mittens on their chilly rats.

The snowflakes twirl, they laugh and play,
Making angels in disarray.
Snowball fights break out and soar,
As hot cocoa spills on the floor.

Under twinkling lights up high,
Even squirrels attempt to fly.
With mischief in their little eyes,
They startle folks with snowy pies.

So let's embrace this winter scene,
With joyous laughter—what a dream!
For every slip upon the ice,
Makes memories that are oh so nice.

Snowflakes and Secrets

Snowflakes fall like whispers soft,
Tickling noses, lifting off.
With every flake, a secret played,
In winter's arms, where fun is made.

Children giggle, cheeks aglow,
Building forts, as wild winds blow.
They stash their candy, cocoa too,
In snowman's pockets, just for you.

Laughter echoes through the trees,
As dancing branches bend with ease.
Snowball stash gets raided fast,
The biggest hit, a snowball blast!

At night when stars begin to peek,
Dreams take flight, and laughter squeaks.
Snowflakes swirling, joy's renown,
As secrets tumble through the town.

Beneath the Pine's Embrace

Underneath the pine's embrace,
Reindeer play a snowy race.
Scraping antlers as they speed,
Finding treasures, oh indeed!

Pinecones tumble, a bumpy ride,
Elfin giggles, full of pride.
They gather 'round a cozy fire,
Toasting marshmallows, never tire.

One brave elf eyes mistletoe,
Underneath the branches low.
But when he leaps to steal a kiss,
He lands face-first—oh, what a miss!

So while the pine trees sway and sway,
We'll wrap up funny tales all day.
In winter's glow, hearts come alive,
With quirky joys that help us thrive.

Carols in the Chill

In the chill, the carols rise,
With joyful songs that fill the skies.
But oh dear me, what's this I hear?
A cat that sings, and takes a leer!

A chorus sung by woofs and meows,
As carol night brings happy vows.
With jingle bells and giggles near,
The funniest sounds rudely cheer.

So gather 'round, the crowd draws near,
For every flat note, there's a cheer!
While snowflakes swirl with tuneful glee,
The warmest hearts are wild and free.

With laughter echoing in the night,
And mischief dancing in the light.
We sing our songs amidst the chill,
As moments blossom, sweet and ill.

A Solstice Serenade

In the glow of twinkling lights,
Socks are hung, oh what a sight,
Cats in hats on the tree,
Who knew they loved festivity?

Chili spills on the snow-white rug,
Grandma dances, gives a shrug,
Elves are now on coffee breaks,
As we plot our holiday shakes.

Cookies gone in just one bite,
Reindeer games take off at night,
Snowmen sing with carrot noses,
While mum's stuck in holiday poses.

Underneath the mistletoe's gaze,
Dancing laughter fills the maze,
Hold your breath for quite the show,
Prepare for chaos, down we go!

Threads of Wonder Woven in White

Snowflakes prance like tiny sprites,
Jumping high, what silly sights,
Scarves and hats all mismatched too,
Fashion tips from a parka crew.

Sleds go racing down the hill,
Cheeks a-ruddy from the chill,
Snowball fights, oh what a blast,
Watch out, or you'll be hit fast!

Laughter echoes through the airs,
Santa laughs at all our snares,
Gingerbread men make a fuss,
Sneak away, let's ride the bus!

Balloons tied to every chair,
What's that smell? It's pumpkin flair,
Every snack we munch and crunch,
Will tumble us with laughter's punch!

Whispers of Frosted Dreams

In a world of frosted cream,
Hot cocoa flows—a tasty dream,
Marshmallows hop on in delight,
As tastebuds dance each chilly night.

Polar bears play peek-a-boo,
With every child as they pass through,
Mittens lost in snowball shock,
There's Uncle Fred—time to mock!

Gifts that jiggle, what's inside?
A sock? A sock? Why must we bide?
Wrap it tight, let's shake and see,
Oh great—it's just more socks for me!

Giggles slip through snowy lanes,
We'll make snow angels with our brains,
Frosted laughter fills the air,
Bouncing joy is everywhere!

The Magic Beneath the Mistletoe

Underneath the leafy sheen,
Two friends plan their silly scheme,
One missed kiss, and now it's fate,
Now everyone's running late!

Grandpa twirls, then takes a spill,
His laughter echoes, what a thrill,
Reindeer dance in kitchen heat,
While Santa tries to find a seat.

Bells of chaos clash and chime,
Is it too late? Do we have time?
A ladder falls, a kitten flies,
Oh what fun! Let's all just try!

Grab the joy, hold it tight,
Spin and twirl, what a sight,
Underneath this playful glow,
Found the magic, don't you know?

Embracing the Spirit of Giving

In a sleigh, old Santa sits,
With tangled lights and candy bits.
His reindeer dance, a wobbly sight,
While Mrs. Claus munches treats tonight.

Gifts wrapped tight in paper bold,
But cats will find them, truth be told.
Each bow a challenge, each box a thrill,
As pets turn joy into sheer mayhem still.

Fuzzy socks and scented soaps,
Pine-scented dreams and silly hopes.
But where's the gift I thought to please?
Turned out it's just more catnip tease!

Yet laughter shared is just the key,
While chaos rules beneath the tree.
For in this crazy, jolly spree,
The gift of joy brings harmony!

Shadows of the Past and Future

Ghosts of holiday past, they cheer,
With mistletoe and lots of beer.
Their funny tales we can't outgrow,
Like Uncle Fred and his disco show.

The future flickers with twinkling lights,
Will we roast a turkey or pizza bites?
As shadows dance on snowflakes bright,
A feast of laughs is our delight.

We ponder gifts, what will they be?
Last year's socks, or maybe a bee?
The future always holds a twist,
Could be a gift we can't resist!

From yesteryears and dreams ahead,
We weave a path for fun instead.
In every giggle, every prank,
We find a joy, our hearts are thankful!

The Colors of a Festive Heart

Red and green, it's a merry sight,
With funky hats and lights so bright.
We paint the town with laughter's cheer,
While carolers sing with no sense of fear!

Ornaments hang with stories to tell,
Of aunties who dance and relatives who fell.
The colors blend like a fruitcake bake,
With nuts and sprinkles for goodness' sake!

The laughter rolls like snowballs thrown,
With holiday quirks we've always known.
Mismatched socks on chilly toes,
We strut our stuff like pros in rows!

Yet in the mess, our hearts find grace,
In every giggle, a warm embrace.
For what's a feast without a jest,
To celebrate this colorful quest!

Frosty Melodies of Delight

In the frosty air, a tune is spun,
Where snowflakes crash in a joyful run.
Silly snowmen with wobbly hats,
Tell jokes to mice and chubby rats.

The city glows, a gleeful sight,
With laughter bubbling through the night.
We dance in circles, trip on ice,
Trying our best, though not so nice!

With cocoa warm, and whipped cream tall,
We sip and giggle, tip, and sprawl.
Who knew that snow could bring such cheer,
As friendly snowballs sail near here?

So let's embrace this frosty play,
With every tumble, a bright array.
In melodies that bubble anew,
We find delight in all we do!

Stardust on Evergreen

In the forest deep and wide,
A tree stood tall, it swayed with pride.
With ornaments hanging, a sight so grand,
A squirrel in a hat, conducting a band.

Tinsel sparkled like stars above,
While reindeer danced, oh what a love!
Gifts piled high, but none were caught,
A present-wrapped cat, now that's just fraught!

Trees in the night, they shimmer and shine,
As carols are sung, and eggnog's divine.
A cupcake's hijinks, frosting on nose,
While snowball fights end in giggles and dose.

Silent night, but wait, what's that?
A raccoon, with style, dressed in a hat!
He's got the moves, he's stealing the show,
Dancing with joy, twirling in snow!

An Evening of Magic and Light

In the glow of lights, the fun begins,
Gingerbread men sporting silly grins.
A candle snickers, a garland giggles,
While Santa's belly jiggled with wiggles.

Reindeer games on rooftops abound,
With sleighs doing flips, oh such a sound!
Mittens mismatched, the fashion's a blast,
While cocoa spills, oh what a contrast.

Elves with clappers, at work in delight,
Wrapping up laughter through the night.
But one pair of socks, what a shocking sight,
They had a party, and surely took flight!

Sparkles in the air, laughter erupts,
As snowmen rejoice in their carrot cups.
With giggles so loud, exuberance flies,
It's a night of mishaps, laughter, and pies!

Echoes of Joy in the Snow

The snowflakes whisper as they dance,
While kids in mittens take a chance.
A penguin slips, oh what a fall!
And snowball battles? They're having a ball!

Hot cocoa's brewing, marshmallows afloat,
As grandma's cat steals one cozy coat.
Laughter unwinds on a frozen pond,
As slippers glide, oh what's beyond?

With snowmen grinning, and hats askew,
A cat in a scarf says, 'Look at you!'
With scarves tied tight, in colorful hues,
Tripping on flavors of gingerbread chews.

The evening rolls on, with giggles and growls,
Hot cider spills, the laughter howls!
In the sparkle of lights, stories unfold,
As joy echoes in the winter so bold.

The Lasting Warmth of Yuletide

In the warmth of the hearth, a flame takes flight,
Puppies tumble, getting tangled with delight.
Grandpa's snoring, his chair tilts back,
While the ornaments giggle, holding their knack.

The cookies vanish, a big surprise,
As elves trade winks with mischievous eyes.
Mom's Christmas sweater, it's bright and loud,
With a unicorn on it, she feels so proud!

Sledding down hills on a donut-shaped tire,
With grin-soaked faces that never tire.
Fuzzy socks sliding on wooden floors,
As grandkids race in a vibrant uproar.

Festivities whirl, and wrapping unspools,
A mystery box of odd-shaped jewels.
Yet laughter's the gift that we treasure so dear,
As memories sparkle throughout the year!

Glimmers of Hope in the Cold

In the fridge, the leftovers play,
Hiding from light, avoiding decay.
A turkey leg wears a sad frown,
While gravy dreams of a royal crown.

The snowman's nose has been borrowed,
From the carrot stew we once swallowed.
He smiles through frost, a goofy prank,
With a hat like a ship, adrift in a tank.

Mittens are dancing with jittery feet,
As squirrels watch, nudging their treat.
A warm mug of cocoa swirls around,
Whipped cream mustache is holiday bound.

The cat's in the tree, just swinging by,
With ornaments plucked, oh my, oh my!
And who knew pine-scented laughter could grow,
In the fluff of the flakes that twinkle below?

Lanterns of Hope

The candles are wobbling like a pair of clowns,
Painting shadows on walls and upside-down towns.
Each flicker a giggle, each flame a small joke,
While Aunt Edna chokes on the holiday smoke.

Pinecones wear hats, it's a cozy affair,
While cookies conspire to vanish from air.
The elves in the attic throw dust from their stash,
Turning flour into magic with every big splash.

At midnight the lights, they start to all hum,
Like a chorus of critters, oh here they come!
With a dash of delight, the night barters cheer,
For the joy that is waiting, it's finally here!

A reindeer hiccups, it's quite a sight,
As Rudolph's nose blinks in the still of the night.
The snowflakes are laughing, the stars join the spree,
While cozy blankets whisper their secret decree.

The Dance of the North Wind

The north wind arrived with a wicked grin,
Twirling the leaves and a wayward pin.
With snowflakes as dancers, they took to the floor,
While Grandma's old scarf escapes through the door.

Frosty knees knocking, the chill does a spin,
As snowmen conspire with mischievous grins.
A jolly old hat bobs to and fro,
With a broomstick partner, putting on a show.

The hot cocoa bubbles with laughter and cheer,
As marshmallows tumble without any fear.
Gingerbread houses sway to the sound,
Of jolly old footsteps that leap all around.

And when the dawn breaks, the giggles entwine,
With laughter like ribbons all wrapped in twine.
The north wind chuckles, it's all just a game,
As the world turns its head to the winter's acclaim.

A Symphony of Sparkles

A symphony rises with each sparkly flake,
As carolers mingle, their voices awake.
The gingerbread men start to tap their thin shoes,
While eggnog concocts its delightful sweet muse.

It's a concert of chaos in the light of the tree,
Where tinsel clashes like a wild jubilee.
The cat plays the violin with strings made of yarn,
While the dogs joined in, woofing songs that they churn.

With ornaments jingling, a raucous refrain,
As sugarplums prance through the frosty domain.
And all the cookies feel quite out of place,
While giggling marshmallows dance in their grace.

Toasting to jesters, a toast with a twist,
For the season of laughter is one we can't miss.
So grab all your friends, come join in the fun,
As the symphony sparkles till the day is done!

Lights Dancing on Winter's Canvas

Twinkling bulbs on the trees,
A squirrel skating with ease!
Snowflakes giggle as they fall,
Nature's ball, it's a free-for-all!

Baking cookies, I burned a batch,
Smoky scent, what a crazy catch!
Rudolph's nose, a glowing flare,
He's just hopeful, finding a chair!

Mittens mismatched, a fashion fright,
But who cares? We'll dance tonight!
Hot cocoa spills, the dog just grins,
Let's toast to the wobbly wins!

With laughter ringing, joy ablaze,
We'll jingle all in quirky ways!
So here's to winter, full of glee,
And all the silly antics we see!

A Tapestry of Yuletide Joy

Gather 'round the festive table,
Is that Uncle Joe, or a fable?
Snowman wearing a funky hat,
With carrot nose—what's up with that?

Pointy ears and a twisty grin,
Santa's lost—hop on, let's spin!
Cookies gone, oh what a crime,
The elves danced, oh how sublime!

Presents piled in a jumbled heap,
Bowing down as the cat takes a leap!
Wrapping paper and ribbons fly,
Oh my, the dog just gave us the eye!

Count the days with a quirky cheer,
Let's toast to laughter and festive beer!
With silly friends, all in tow,
This tapestry of joy steals the show!

The Magic of Gifting Hearts

Surprise! A box of socks for me!
Just what I wanted—how could it be?
Wrapped in paper, tied with flair,
Who knew that socks could cause such despair?

Gift exchanges turn into a game,
"Let's just swap—who's really to blame?"
A cat in a scarf, oh what a sight,
He could outshine the twinkling lights!

Grandma's secret, a fruitcake delight,
"Two years old, but still just right!"
We'll share a slice with a wink and grin,
Because what's the harm in mixing it in?

So here's to giving, with laughter and glee,
Gifting our hearts, come dance, you and me!
Silly presents wrapped with heart,
Who knew that magic could come from a part?

Silent Nights and Shimmering Lights

On silent nights, we cause a ruckus,
As carolers sing out of pure focus!
The tree's too tall, it touches the sky,
Look out, we're all about to fly!

Jingle bells and a snowman race,
Each tumble provides an amusing chase!
Snowflakes swirl, then down we go,
Landing softly, laughter in tow!

Candles flicker in a charming dance,
Who lit that one? The puppy's at a glance!
With sassy hats, we twirl in bliss,
This merry season, can you resist?

So join the mirth, the giggles alight,
For in this magic, we take flight!
With shimmering lights igniting cheer,
We'll laugh and play, all through the year!

Stillness and Sparkle

In the quiet of night, not a sound,
But a gift's rattle makes laughter abound.
Tinsel on the cat makes him a star,
He struts like he knows he's gone far.

Cookies left out, a daring delight,
Who brings crumbs? It's the elf with no sight!
Reindeer hooves dance on the roof with glee,
While Santa's stuck, shouting, "Oh, let me be!"

The tree sways slowly, a giant in dreams,
Toppled by kids and a few too many beams.
Glittery chaos in the holiday cheer,
With snowflakes giggling as they draw near.

So let's wrap it in laughter, not dread,
For joy comes with every misstep we've led.
And the sparkle we find in our silly mistakes,
Makes the stillness a wonder that simply awakes.

A Hearth's Glove in Winter's Grasp

The fire is crackling, but so is my toast,
With marshmallows flying, they're not what I boast.
The mittens are stuck, where's my right hand?
Hearth's glove in a tussle, oh, what a grand stand!

Socks on the floor seem to dance and parade,
While hot cocoa spills, and the kids are dismayed.
The cat takes a leap, a dramatic flair,
Catches the garland, now I just stare.

Snowflakes are wrestled, they melt on my nose,
While I chase down the toddler with candy cane woes.
Laughter erupts like the bubbles in tea,
As we snuggle together, just dad, mom, and me.

So we sit by the fire, with giggles in tow,
Warmed hearts like embers, all aglow.
Though winter may grasp us in chilly embrace,
We find warmth in laughter, no cold can replace.

Whirlwinds of Yuletide Memories

Whirlwinds of memories twirl in the air,
Like ornaments flying without a care.
The reindeer are plotting a snowball surprise,
While Santa's stuck munching—oh, what a guise!

Mittens are misplaced, like socks starting fights,
Gifts under the tree have mysterious heights.
The dog leapt for joy, took the wrapping away,
And now it's a game of 'who stole my sleigh?'

Tinsel wraps around, the lights start to blink,
While up in the attic, dad's having a drink.
With laughter as bright as the star on the tree,
We bask in the mayhem, just happy to be.

So gather your loved ones, with humor and cheer,
The whirlwind of joy comes 'round every year.
In memories made, both the silly and sweet,
We discover the magic in the chaos we greet.

The Language of Bundled Joy

In the language of joy, we bundle it tight,
With laughter and giggles that dance through the night.
Wrapping up stories like gifts yet untold,
As the mischief of children finds treasures of old.

Footprints in snow lead to cookies astray,
While Santa's sleigh jingles—oh, what a display!
The puppy is tangled in ribbons and bows,
Rolling like snowballs while everyone glows.

Bells jingle loudly, a delightful mess,
As we stumble through chaos, we still feel blessed.
With each joyful moment, we continue to pile,
A language of laughter that stretches a mile.

So let us all gather, both near and afar,
With handmade joy as our guiding star.
In the warmth of togetherness, spirits will soar,
The bundle of laughter—our loved ones adore.

Secrets Hidden in the Snow

Beneath the snow, secrets lie,
A snowman's hat, a lopsided eye.
He tells tall tales when no one's near,
Of nights spent dancing, full of cheer.

Snowflakes drift, some land on noses,
Penguins in hats strike silly poses.
Children giggle at the sight,
While sledding down in pure delight.

Footprints lead to a hidden stash,
Where snowballs build and friendships clash.
But who can tell what stories are spun,
In the frosty fun of the winter sun?

Jingle bells ring in a frosty chime,
As laughter echoes through snowball crime.
The secrets of snow, they always know,
In a world where wonders forever grow.

Wishes on a Winter Breeze

Whispers fly on a chilly breeze,
Santa's sleigh brings smiles with ease.
A wish for socks that don't feel tight,
And cookies that glow with pure delight.

Icicles hang like nature's bling,
While snowflakes dance, oh how they sing!
Every wish wrapped in frosted lace,
Bringing giggles to every face.

Hot cocoa spills in a cheerful mess,
With marshmallows that make us all confess:
We'd trade our toys for a snowball fight,
And giggle till late into the night.

Wishes float on the winter air,
With laughter echoing everywhere.
Each little dream, a flurry of glee,
On a breeze where we long to be free.

The Gift of Laughter

The best gift isn't wrapped with care,
It's laughter shared, beyond compare.
With silly jokes and playful puns,
It sparkles more than shiny tons.

A reindeer dance in the living room,
While dad trips over the vacuum's plume.
Mom's sweet giggle is the sweetest sound,
As joy and chaos all around.

Jingle all the way to funny tales,
With hot cocoa and buttery trails.
The gift of laughter, oh so bright,
Turns winter days into sheer delight.

So hang a smile upon that tree,
String up some jokes, just wait and see.
With every chuckle, your spirits will lift,
For laughter's truly the brightest gift.

Memories Wrapped in Seasons

In each season, fun reflections tease,
Falling snowflakes carried by the breeze.
Mistletoe mischief, a kiss or two,
With giggles nearby, who knew?

Fireside tales of past delight,
Where socks were hung every Christmas night.
Stories of antics, pranks galore,
Wrapped in warmth, we all adore.

Frosty faces and snowball fights,
With hot cider on cozy nights.
Every moment, a treasure trove,
In these seasons, we learn to love.

Memories twinkle like stars above,
Each laugh a blanket, warm and snug.
Package them tight in a heart's embrace,
For every season holds its grace.

Echoes of Laughter in the Frost

Snowflakes dance without a care,
A penguin slips, it's quite a scare.
Do reindeer really fly this high?
Squeals of giggles fill the sky.

Frosty tried to feel his nose,
But ended up in snow-like prose.
Hot cocoa served with a splash,
Watch out world, here comes the crash!

With joy and jests, we cheer and sing,
Decking halls with every fling.
Even the elves are in on the game,
All wrapped up in holiday fame!

So gather 'round with mirth and cheer,
Silly hats and snacks are here.
In this chilly world of white,
We laugh and play through the night.

Moments Lost in Mistletoe

Hanging high, that sprig of green,
Underneath, a silly scene.
A cat that leaps, a dog that barks,
Kissing chaos, oh what larks!

Everyone's sneaking for a smooch,
But Auntie Jane's the biggest hootch.
Right at the moment, she trips and stumbles,
With gingerbread men and laughter, it tumbles.

The clock strikes twelve, oh what a fuss,
Grandpa starts singing without a plus.
The mistletoe's snaring all in sight,
As giggles erupt into pure delight!

Such moments are treasures, so they say,
Laughter keeps the blues at bay.
Underneath that festive bloom,
We create a joyful, happy room!

The Spirit of Giving Unveiled

Boxes piled up, a curious sight,
But peek inside and, oh what fright!
Socks for the dog and hats for tea,
Who would give such things to me?

A gift of fruitcake lies in wait,
Is it love, or just plain fate?
When re-gifting becomes an art,
Laughter and cheer fill each heart.

The kids are crafting gifts of cheer,
Made of glitter, glue, and sheer.
With crooked bows and paint on hands,
They giggle, oh, at their own plans!

So here's to what we choose to share,
Bizarre and funny, full of flair.
In this time of giving and delight,
We'll laugh together, shining bright!

Candles Flickering in Stillness

Candles glow with playful flicks,
Casting shadows that do tricks.
A puppy sniffs at waxy cheer,
Then promptly sneezes, oh my dear!

The carolers sing with all their might,
But one forgot the words tonight.
Off-key notes fill up the night,
And yet we laugh, it's pure delight.

Sledding down a snowy street,
Laughter echoes, so sweet, so neat.
A snowman falls, a brutal blow,
With laughter loud, we watch it go!

In the stillness, magic swells,
With every giggle, warmth compels.
Candles flicker, hearts grow fonder,
In this season, we laugh, we wander.

Glistening Horizons of Cheer

In a snowman suit, he danced around,
With carrot nose, he fell to the ground.
Under twinkling lights, not a creature was sad,
Even the cat joined, doing the rad!

Cookies on plates all piled up high,
Santas in pajamas not even shy.
A sleigh team of reindeer flew right by,
But they stopped for some cocoa 'cause oh my!

Giggles erupted from rooftops they soared,
As elves made the toys, not one was ignored.
A gift wrapped in sparkles fell onto my head,
Turns out it was just a sock full of dread!

Oh, the laughter, oh, the glee,
Will the penguin please hand me my tea?
With each little blunder, we all roll our eyes,
In this world of chaos, joy never dies!

The Village of Dreams and Light

In the village square, the lights shone bright,
But watch that tree stand, it wobbles just right!
A mad dash of children, their cheeks full of pie,
Chasing a dog who thinks it can fly!

Baking went wrong, flour flew like snow,
Mom's gingerbread man now has a flat toe.
Each bite brings a giggle, it tastes quite a lot
Like grandma's old slippers, still warm from the pot!

The townsfolk are singing, off-key, but loud,
While costumes of reindeer draw in a crowd.
Oh wait, there's a chicken, or was it a duck?
These holiday antics? Just plain dumb luck!

At the end of the day, when the laughter does fade,
A moon made of cheese serves up the charade.
Together we gather, and under the stars,
Our hearts filled with joy, as goofy as ours!

Of Miracles and Moonlit Nights

When magic arrives with a grin and a bow,
My slippers are missing—oh, where did they go?
A reindeer appeared with a wink and a cheer,
Said, "Dance with me, buddy, your slippers are here!"

Lights hung on rooftops like spaghetti of glow,
Neighbors are arguing 'bout which way to throw.
The snowflakes are swirling, they're plotting a scheme,
To bury the snowman while we all dream!

Gifts wrapped in paper made more for a jest,
A cat hides inside, it's turned into a fest.
We unwrap all the laughter and giggles that brighten,
As our faces are glowing, the fun is both frighten!

As night turns to dawn, there's a shiver of glee,
With rumors of magic, oh just wait and see!
A sock on my foot feels joy like a flight,
As I twirl through this wonder, on moonlit nights!

Whims of the Winter Wind

The winter wind whispers of giggles and glee,
It tickles the noses of all, can you see?
A penguin in boots waddles near the toy shop,
While a snowball brigade makes the laughter go pop!

Hot cocoa is splashed as we frolic around,
The marshmallows fly in a soft puffy cloud.
An igloo of laughter is building so bright,
As the little ones chase, acting silly tonight!

Snowflakes as poppers fall softly and sweet,
While the dogs spin about on their wobbly feet.
A round of good cheer bundled up in big fluff,
Says the wind through the smiles, "Oh, isn't this fun?"

As jingle bells jangle, we dance through the snow,
Each silly old move takes us high with the flow.
In this wind of whimsy, oh what a delight,
Together we laugh in the glow of the night!

Chasing Softly Falling Snow

Little flakes on my nose, oh what fun,
I catch one to eat, it tastes like a bun.
Snowball fights break out in the park,
With laughter and giggles, we leave our mark.

Pigeons waddle by, they give quite a stare,
As I slip on ice, do a dance in the air.
My scarf flies away like a launched paper plane,
I chase it in circles, oh what a gain!

Neighbors build forts, with mugs in their hands,
While I'm stuck outside, making snowmen with bands.
The carrot nose grins, a snowman rides high,
I'll claim it's my cousin, to my mom I'll lie.

Yet when dusk paints the sky a shimmering blue,
We gather and sing, silly songs—just a few.
As stars peek out, giving twinkles all around,
We dive into laughter, pure joy is found.

Ribbons of Light Dancing

Tinsel and sparkles, oh what a sight,
I trip over cords in the glow of the night.
The tree stands tall, but it leans to the right,
As ornaments giggle, hiding out of sight.

Mittens are matched, but none are the same,
Trying to find them is quite the wild game.
The dog plays with ribbons, oh what a delight,
He pirouettes clumsily, stealing the light.

Kids dash around, with excitement they hum,
Wrapping up presents, oh, this is so fun!
Tape sticks to my fingers, I'm tangled up tight,
As I wrestle the paper—a glorious fight.

Finally, we toast with mugs raised up high,
While laughter erupts, the spirits can fly.
With cookies and jokes we dance all about,
In this silly chaos, there's no room for doubt.

A Hearth of Warmth and Wonder

The fire pops and crackles, with marshmallows in hand,
I start roasting socks—oh no! That was unplanned.
The laughter erupts, as we all shake our heads,
Guess I'm having toast instead of fresh breads.

Hot cocoa is spilt, but it makes quite a show,
With chocolate mustaches, we're all in the know.
Grandpa tells stories of things long ago,
With ghosts in the mix, we all scream, "Oh no!"

Yet here by the hearth, with the warmth on our toes,
Bad jokes are accepted and friendship just grows.
As snow swirls outside like a white fluffy gown,
Inside the giggles bloom, a holiday crown.

The night wraps around us like a blanket of cheer,
We laugh and we dance, 'til the morning draws near.
With hearts full of joy and stumbles galore,
We'll treasure these moments, forever encore!

The Joy of Whispering Pines

Under the pines where the whispers arise,
I trip over roots, oh what a surprise!
The scent of fresh needles tickles my nose,
While squirrels in sweaters put on a great show.

Adventurers call me, "Come play with us here!"
So I tumble and fumble, filled up with good cheer.
With pine cones for hats, we're quite the fun crew,
Even if some join in—just little and blue!

The paths lead us straight to a frozen wide lake,
Where we slide and we glide, oh make no mistake!
The awkward little penguins, they steal all our grace,
As we wobble and tumble, each laugh finds its place.

We gather by fires, the night sings its charms,
Roasting up snacks with old tales where disarms.
In the joy of these pines, we find magic anew,
With laughter and wonder, all sparkles come through.

Beneath the Stars, We Gather

Beneath twinkling stars, we congregate,
With mugs of warm cocoa, we celebrate.
The dog barks at shadows, thinking they're mice,
While the cat just rolls over, not moving a slice.

We wear silly hats, each one more absurd,
And share cheesy jokes, not one will be heard.
With cookies ablaze, the oven erupts,
As we laugh 'til we snort, our stomachs all clumped.

The snowflakes are falling, each one is unique,
Just like Uncle Bob's dance, which is far from chic.
We giggle at stories of past holiday woes,
Like when Aunt May's fruitcake had no one to pose.

Beneath the night sky, our spirits take flight,
With joy in each corner, our hearts feel so light.
In this cozy chaos, love's weaving its thread,
As we cherish these moments, and the laughter we've bred.

Threads of Gold in the Night

Amidst shimmering lights, we thread our own fate,
With glittering tinsel that never looks straight.
The dog found the garland, it's now on his head,
And Grandma's lost glasses, on top of the bread.

We string up the bulbs, they flicker and sway,
A few even wink, like they're here for the play.
A lively debate on which eggnog's the best,
As we sip from our cups, the chill we invest.

With giggles and hiccups, we tumble and fall,
And the tree topples over—oh dear, yikes, not at all!
Yet the chaos brings warmth, like a hug from the past,
With threads of our laughter, these moments will last.

So here we are, misfits, together we shine,
With memories fashioned from chaos divine.
In the night filled with wonder, we sing out our tune,
Blasting holiday cheer beneath the big moon.

The Embrace of Stories Untold

Around the warm fire, we spin wondrous tales,
About how grandpa Jim chased his tail in stale jails.
With marshmallows just burning, a sight oh-so-out,
While we burst into laughter, we can't help but shout.

The cocoa is swirling, it's now more like goo,
Adding laughter to voices, oh what can we do?
And cousin Lou fell back, 'cause he tried to impress,
As we point at his antics, his utter distress.

With tales misremembered, each plot is a mess,
As we fumble through stories, causing more stress.
Yet somehow the warmth in our hearts overrides,
In this magical moment, where laughter resides.

So let's raise our mugs to the sweetest of nights,
To stories, to laughter, and all of our plights.
With an embrace of joy, let the season take hold,
For the love that we share is a treasure untold.

Lanterns Adrift on Snowfall

As lanterns float gently, they dance in the breeze,
Mismatched and quirky, with laughter that frees.
The snowflakes will twirl, and the kids, oh what fun,
With snowballing antics, they race 'til they're done.

A squirrel named Carl steals a peanut or two,
While we giggle and stare, 'What's a critter to do?'
The snowman looks worried, his carrot's askew,
As he turns to complain, that our aim's gotten skewed.

Lanterns aglow, they illuminate cheer,
As we chase all our worries, and toast to the year.
With silly traditions, we dance in the cold,
In the warmth of our laughter, true magic unfolds.

So here's to the joy, let's cherish it bright,
With lanterns afloat, we'll embrace the delight.
Next year may be wild, it's a life we will savor,
Wrapped in each giggle, a moment of flavor.

Snowflakes Whispering Secrets

Snowflakes dance with silly grace,
Tickling noses, making a face.
They giggle as they land on me,
Silly whispers, oh what glee!

Kids bundled up, a colorful sight,
Building snowmen, oh what a plight!
One's got a carrot, the other's a mop,
A lopsided grin, we just can't stop!

Snowball fights in laughter's cheer,
Cheers and chuckles, loud and clear.
Yet one blob flies and misses its mark,
Hits Dad instead, oh what a lark!

Winter nights with cocoa delight,
Marshmallows bobbing, oh what a sight!
Sipping slowly as stories unfold,
Snowflakes whisper the warmth we hold.

The Glimmer of Starlit Nights

Stars wink brightly, oh what jest,
Dancing above in their sparkly best.
One falls down, lands on the tree,
A wishful twinkle just for me!

The moon's a lantern, round and bright,
Stirring laughter in the night.
It says, 'Don't trip on the reindeer shine!'
As we stumble and giggle, feeling divine!

Crisp air filled with snickering sounds,
Jingle bells ringing all around.
'Wait, is that a sleigh I can hear?'
No, just Uncle Joe, in high holiday cheer!

When the world is wrapped in hushed delight,
Magic unfolds on a starry night.
With every twinkle, joy seems to grow,
In the merry chaos, we let laughter flow.

Festive Dreams in Frosted Air

Frosty windows, a sight to behold,
Dreams wrapped in stories, soft and bold.
Elves in pajamas, what a funny view,
Sipping hot cocoa, feeling brand new!

Pine-scented whispers fill the room,
As we giggle at snowmen's costume.
A twirly hat, socks mismatched,
A jolly jumble that's proudly hatched!

Sleigh bells ring with a jingling tune,
Uncle dons antlers, quite a buffoon.
'Tis the season for merriment spread,
While laughter dances around our heads!

Dancing in socks on polished floors,
Sliding and jumping, just like before.
With every fall, the giggles grow loud,
Amid frosted dreams, we sing out proud!

Under the Evergreen's Embrace

Beneath the branches, oh what a sight,
Squirrels playing, full of delight.
One clumsily drops an acorn or two,
Sneaky giggles echo, as they pursue!

Ornaments hang like tasty treats,
While pets sniff at these festive feats.
A gingerbread men chase on the floor,
'Twas a cookie slip, now they're wanting more!

Under the twinkle of lights overhead,
Family stories and laughter are spread.
Stealing a cookie, with crumbs on the cheek,
In this wild season, it's joy that we seek!

The air fills with cheer, and laughter we share,
Spreading smiles, as love fills the air.
In the embrace of evergreens tall,
Life's funny moments bring joy to us all!

Tales from the Snowy Lane

In snowy fields where snowmen dance,
A carrot nose gives them a chance.
The kids all cheer, with hats askew,
As snowballs fly, laughter ensues.

But wait! What's that? A sled takes flight!
It bumps a tree, what a silly sight!
With giggles loud, they tumble down,
In a snowy heap, all giggles and frowns.

The dog runs by, a fluffy blur,
Chasing a snowflake, what a stir!
He dives and rolls, oh what fun!
A flurry of fur, he's on the run!

Then comes a break for cocoa warm,
With marshmallows big, the perfect charm.
They sip and sip, their cheeks aglow,
Planning more antics, off they go!

A Chorus of Merry Hearts

In the kitchen, pots a-clang,
Mom's singing loud, her voice goes twang!
Cookies baked with sprinkles bright,
Dad's in charge of the oven's light.

The cat jumps up, the flour's flight,
Paws in the dough, oh what a sight!
With whiskers dusted, he starts to purr,
A furry chef in a festive blur!

The kids all giggle, with dough on their cheeks,
They dance around, full of squeaks.
The chorus builds, a joyful sound,
With flour fights and laughs abound!

And as the bake-off comes to close,
They stuff their faces, goodness knows!
With crumbs galore and hearts so light,
Who knew kitchen chaos could be so bright?

The Serenity of Candlelight

Candle flames flicker, dancing slow,
As shadows stretch, putting on a show.
But then a breeze, from nowhere blows,
And out go lights—oh, how it glows!

The kids all squeal, the room's a fright,
They grab their flashlights, what a sight!
With beams of joy, they start to play,
Imitating stars, in their own way.

Mom lights a match, with a gentle sigh,
Creating warmth, and whoosh, they fly!
With giggles and gasps, they form a ring,
Embracing the magic that candles bring.

But candles need care, or so they say,
One flick and they could melt away!
So they join hands, a silly parade,
With waxy warriors, they're unafraid!

Blessings Wrapped in Gold

Underneath the tree, the gifts do sit,
Wrapped in bows, each one a hit!
But what's this? A box so wide,
With giggles contained, they can't abide.

It's marked for Dad, he shakes it slow,
"What's in this box? I'm dying to know!"
With each small jiggle, he starts to grin,
But as he sneaks a peek, they all begin!

The kids shout "No!" while all in fun,
As Dad's attempt to sneak is done!
With laughter loud, he joins the chase,
Around the tree, it's a funny race!

Finally, he stops, they catch their breath,
With hugs so tight, the joy's no less.
Blessings in gold, but laughter's the best,
With hearts so full, they know they're blessed!

Frost-Kissed Wishes

Tiny elves on sugar roofs,
Skid on icing, what a goof!
Pine tree wobbles, tinsel flies,
Caught the cat right by surprise.

Cookies stacked in towering heaps,
Milk mustache while Santa sleeps.
Snagged his list, oh what a sight—
Naughty giggles in the night.

Frosty noses, laughter loud,
Snowballs tossed, we feel so proud.
With each splash, a joyful cheer,
Winter's antics bring us near.

Wrapping paper flies around,
Ribbons tangled on the ground.
In the chaos, we all roar,
Who knew this is what fun's for?

The Secret of Silent Nights

Miracle in the quiet air,
Socks are hiding—oh, beware!
Candles flicker, shadows dance,
Step on tinsel? Take the chance!

Whispers of holiday delight,
Gingerbread men take to flight.
One gets caught up in the door,
Crumbs left behind, forevermore!

Rudolph's nose is in a plight,
Leads the sleigh in sheer moonlight.
Santa's laugh shakes all the trees,
Better watch out for those knees!

Stocking stuffer? Left behind!
Sneak peeks—oh, what do we find?
Lumps of coal? Or candy treats?
What a conundrum, it repeats!

Radiant Echoes of Goodwill

Hooey and laughter fill the hall,
Someone's slipped and starts to fall.
Belly shakes with every chuckle,
Presents lost in Christmas shuffle.

Wrapping paper, colorful mess,
In a twist, we've all confessed.
What would happen if we dare,
Wear those bows right in our hair?

Midnight snacks all disappear,
Cookie crumbs and soda cheer.
Oops! That pie is gone for sure,
Guess we'll bake another—more!

Festive hats and mismatched socks,
Dance around with jolly knocks.
Echoes of laughter fill the space,
In this wild and cheerful race!

Bells Ringing Through the Haze

Jingle bells—a silly tune,
Dancing round with goofy boon.
Who slipped on snow? It was me!
Laughter bubbles, can't you see?

Neighbors peeking through their blinds,
Wondering what mischief binds.
Suddenly a carol plays,
We can't help but join the craze!

Hot cocoa spills on my lap,
Wearing marshmallows like a cap.
Sledding down with a woeful cheer,
After I finish this mug, oh dear!

With each clang and every cheer,
Joyous vibes throughout the year.
Oh, the wonders we unfold,
In this merry tale retold!

Milton Keynes UK
Ingram Content Group UK Ltd.
UKHW021241191124
451300UK00007B/179

9 789916 940723